The Joy of Living
Manifesting a Peaceful, Purposeful & Positive You

by

Terri L. McCrea, M.Ed., LPC

The Joy of Living: Manifesting a Peaceful, Purposeful & Positive You

All rights reserved. Unless otherwise noted, no part of this book may be reproduced in any form, except brief reviews, without written permission of the publisher.

Cassaundra Mulligan, Editor

ISBN: 978-1-7355737-5-5

Cover and interior arrangements - by Kathrine Rend
Rend Graphics www.rendgraphics.com

Printed in the United States of America.

Poetic Expressions by Terri
Terri L. McCrea, M.Ed., LPC, LPC/S
1643 B Savannah Highway, #113
Charleston, SC 29407
Mobile (843) 437-7572/Fax (843) 763-7202

poeticexpressions@att.net

The Joy of Living

Manifesting a Peaceful, Purposeful & Positive You

Dedication

    I dedicate this book to my heroes, my family, my friends and my village. I encourage all to use their gifts to inspire hope in this world.

Introduction

To live free and in peace, refrain from I should've, I can't, I won't and I'm not into present centered, future focused and inspiring mantras.

Retrain your brain by utilizing the below mantras to combat negative, self-doubting and self-defeating self-talk.

When Hurt or Scarred, say this Mantra
— I am Healed.

When Disappointed, say this Mantra
— I am Satisfied, I am Grateful and I am Okay.

When feeling Incomplete or Empty, say this Mantra
— I am Complete and Whole.

When Frustrated, say this Mantra
— I am a Go-Getter and Patient.

When Confused, say this Mantra
— I am Confident and I Can Ask for Help.

When Restless, say this Mantra
 – I am Calm and Safe.

When feeling Rejected, say this Mantra
 – I Accept Me and I am Loved.

When Stressed, Anxious or Overwhelmed, say this Mantra
 – I am in Charge of my Peace.

When Dejected, Hopeless or Depressed, say this Mantra
 – I am Joyful and Resilient.

When feeling Inferior, Unimportant or Not Good Enough, say this Mantra
 – I am Capable and Worthy.

When feeling Mistrust, say this Mantra
 – I am Faithful.

When feeling Humiliation or Shame, say this Mantra
 – I am Favored and Proud of Myself.

When feeling Unworthy, say this Mantra
 – I am Deserving.

When feeling Inadequate, say this Mantra
 – I am Able and Good Enough.

When Angry or Revengeful, say this Mantra
 – I am in Control.

When Broken or Bitter, say this Mantra
 – I am Blessed.

When feeling Insecure, Incapable or Fearful, say this Mantra
– I am Courageous.

When feeling Helpless, say this Mantra
– I am Not Alone.

When feeling like a Burden or Not Needed, say this Mantra
– I am Valuable.

When feeling like a Mistake, Unwanted or Disposable, say this Mantra
– I am a Gift.

If you were raised in a home where patriarchs didn't role model chivalry, empathy, bravery, humility, gratefulness, honor, devotion or forgiveness, doesn't mean you can't be that hero, that rock and that leader. You, as a king, can now give yourself permission to live an enriched, meaningful and distinctive life.

If you were raised in a home where matriarchs didn't role model serenity, tenacity, empowerment, strength, compassion, peace, affection and care, doesn't mean you can't create a life filled with balance and healthy traditions and themes. You, now as an adult, can be that thoughtful, loving and strong Eve. You, as a queen, can now give yourself permission to live a bountiful, beautiful and blossomed life.

Even if you weren't treated like a prince, with unconditional love or like a princess, know that you are good enough, unique and special. Don't waste another breath or heartbeat fighting with or running away from your shadow.

Cherish every second of your miraculous existence through positive, peaceful and purposeful eyes.

The Joy of Living

**Manifesting a Peaceful,
Purposeful & Positive You**

What would you desire to be your legacy?

What did you learn about your self during the COVID 19 pandemic?

Who is in your corner and why?

What do you like about the night?

What impact did your father figure have on your life?

What impact did your mother figure have on your life?

> If you could see and talk to anyone in Heaven, who would they be and why?

Who did you forgive to live in peace?

If you could live anywhere in the world, where would it be and why?

Define faith.

> List your life's dreams and steps to achieve them.

Who is or are your best friends and why?

Define love.
Love is…

Describe moments of strength, resiliency and perseverance.

What do you like to do on rainy days that restore, replenish and speak to your soul?

How are you honoring lost loved ones?

If people knew the real you, what would they be surprised to discover?

What are your gifts?

Define true love.

What are your favorite plants, flowers and trees and why?

> Describe a time you fought for something or someone that really mattered.

What positive things soothe your soul?

> What amazes you about life, the world and people?

What makes a house a home?

> Who are you? If you can't think of things to say, think of what your best friend would say.
> I am…

How will you know when someone is the one?

What things do you desire in life and describe steps to obtain them?

What does a perfect weekend look like?

Who are your guardian angels and why them?

What are your favorite colors and why?

List five to ten traits of a perfect gentleman?

What does a perfect world look like?

How can you make a difference during your lifetime?

What are five to ten traits of an ideal mother?

If you could live forever what would you do?

Have you ever experienced dé·jà vu and what did it mean to you?

Describe ways to show gratitude.

What is your destiny?

What are your favorite music genres and listening tunes?

Have you experienced a miracle and describe how it's impacted your life?

> Do you feel free and if not, how can that become a reality?

> Why is reflection important to higher living?

If you can get on a plane, train, bus, motorcycle or in a hot air balloon, where would you want to go and why?

> What moments, in your mind, in the world and in your life, can never be erased and how did it change you?

What does family mean to you?

Write your love story of your time with your soulmate (from the initial meeting to the present).

Describe your wedding day and what would it look like.

Describe what an ideal marriage would look like.

If you could go back and change anything in your past, would you and why or why not?

What things do you do to practice self-love?

What are your reoccurring dreams and what do you think they mean?

What are your favorite desserts?

Describe a father.

> What things are you discovering
> about yourself along life's way?

What do you love about your partner and how has their presence impacted you?

What are you favorite animals and why?

What motivates your steps?

When did you realize that you are in control of your joy, your happiness and your peace?

___

List your heroes/sheroes and why them?

Where do you see yourself in five years?

> If you were to let go of something, what would it be and why?

How would you want to celebrate your existence?

> When did you realize you were in charge of your thoughts, emotions and actions?

Describe how you stay centered, balanced and grounded.

How did your fears hold you back and what steps can you take to conquer them?

When did you find your voice and how does it feel to walk empowered?

When did you discover your purpose and what is it?

What parts of your life do you feel compelled to share (this can be your memoir/autobiography)?

When did you stop living a lie?

How are you blessed?

> What makes you feel torn and how can you become whole again?

How has insanity ruled your life?

Write your 2020 survival story.

What are your spiritual convictions and how have they strengthened you along your life's journey?

Describe a perfect snow day.

What do you like about yourself?

Define hope.

What life lesson(s) did you learn from broken friendships, failed ventures and broken hearts?

Who is in your village and why?

If you were told you had one year to live what would you do?

If you could only have twenty things in your home, what would they be and why?

> If you could have three granted wishes, what would they be and why?

> What insight, clarity and epiphanies has brought growth in your recent years?

If Jesus appeared on earth today, what questions would you have for him?

I Am

I Am Not You.
I Am Me.

I Am No Longer Blind.
Instead, I Walk in Epiphanies.

I Am Not the Reason for your Insanity.
I Am your Reality.

I Am Not your Fate.
Instead, I'm your Destiny.

I Am Not the Ashes after Volcanic Eruptions.
Instead, I Walk Renewed.

I Am Me. I Am Not You.

I Am Not your Past. I Am your Present.
I Am Not a Danger. Instead, I'm Heaven-sent.

I Am Not a Victim. I Am a Survivor.
I Am Not Damaged or Broken.
Instead, I Walk in Purpose, Love and Faith.

I Am Not your Rescuer or Enabler.
Instead, I'm your Impetus in Wait.

I am Not Invisible.
Instead, I'm a Luminös Star.

I am Not the Remnants after a Storm.
Instead, I'm a Blessing from Above.

I am Not a Burden,
a Mistake or your Pain.
Instead, I'm a Precious Gift like
Quenching Jasmine Rain.

I am Not a Slave.
I Am Free.

I Am Not You.
I Am Me.

Summary

The book can be used to help the reader develop goals for passionate, peaceful and positive living; gain greater insight about their partner; grow in their marriage; build connections in their family; bring closure to their past; define their purpose; establish clear intentions over their life; free themselves from a stagnated mindset; take charge of their steps; break unhealthy cycles; address suppressed or repressed memories; find meaning in their life and give themselves permission to embrace joy.

Mantra

I see my limitlessness.
I see my dreams in crimson suns.
I can climb over any mountain.

Author

Terri McCrea is a native of Charleston, South Carolina. She has provided counseling for the past 31 years (23 years of that in private practice). She graduated from St. Andrews Parish High School and the College of Charleston before receiving her Master's Degree in Clinical Counseling from The Citadel. She is an Adjunct Professor, a Licensed Addiction Counselor, a Licensed Professional Counselor, a Licensed Professional Counselor Supervisor and served as a Continuing Education provider for the South Carolina Board for Licensed Professional Counselors, Social Workers, Marital and Family Therapists, Psychologists and Psycho-educational Specialists. She facilitates vision board, leadership, empowerment, mantra and intentions seminars as well as creative writing, author coaching and life skills camps. She is the Outreach Coordinator of the Old Bethel United Methodist Church's Community Outreach Program.

This platform provides preventative, educational, rehabilitative, counseling, and evangelistic services to the Low Country's at-risk youths, families (including the elderly, poor, imprisoned, homeless, disabled and indigent).

Terri writes mental health articles for local magazines and newspapers. She guest appears for mental health segments on local radio and television networks. She can be described as a coach, counselor, visionary, poet, free spirit and believer that everyone and everything has a purpose. She is a member of the Poetry Society of South Carolina (PSSC), Old Bethel United Methodist Choir, Gamma Xi Omega Chapter of Alpha Kappa Alpha Sorority, Inc., International African American Museum and is a proud aunt and grand aunt.

Terri is available for book signings, charity events, public/motivational speaking engagements, workshop facilitation, interviews, and expert appearances (radio, web, television and podcast) and poetry readings. She has self-published five self-help workbooks, four inspirational guides for couples in love, one parenting guide, four empowering guides for tots/tweens/teens, a book of wedding vows (English/Spanish translation), a mantra and intentions book, a how-to-date book and her first collection of poems (2007-2020).

Poetic Expressions by Terri
1643-B Savannah Hwy, Suite 113,
Charleston, SC 29407
(main) 843.437.7572
(facsimile) 843.763.7202
poeticexpressions@att.net

*Visit: www.btol.com
www.Amazon.com
www.Alibris.com
www.Abebooks.com
www.Booksurge.com

Terri L. McCrea's Books

- *The Power of Forgiveness: A Step by Step Guide on How to Let Go, Move On and Begin Living*
- *A Teacher's Dream: A Goal Setting Guide for Tots and Tweens*
- *Problem Solving One on One: Proactive Tactics for Millennium Youths*
- *The Joy of Living: Manifesting a Passionate, Purposeful and Positive You*
- *I Will Be...Inspirational Quotes from Women on the Move, in Love and Standing in their Purpose*
- *I Will Be... Inspirational Quotes from Men on the Move, in Love and Standing in their Purpose*
- *What Women Want to Hear {not just} on Valentine's Day but Everyday*
- *How to Stroke the Male Ego: Words that Make your Man feel like a King*
- *It's Ok for Boys to…*
- *It's Ok for Girls to…*
- *Intentions*
- *The Joy of Living: 20 Steps to a New Beginning*
- *The Book of Mantras: 100 Affirmations to Reframe your Thoughts and Retrain your Brain*
- *Walk Like a King: 100 Virtues of a True Gentleman*
- *Elite Girls Wear Pearls: 100 Virtues of Strong, Empowered and Balanced Women*
- *Soul Encounters: The Collective Poetry of Terri L. McCrea (2007-2020)*
- *Walking in Love: Wedding Vows for that Special Day*
- *2003. 2004, 2nd Edition 2008, What Price Are You Willing to Pay for Love? (Author house: ISBN: 1-418-6299-3 (e-book)/ISBN: 1-4184-3315-2 (Paperback)*

www.ingramcontent.com/pod-product-compliance
Lightning Source LLC
LaVergne TN
LVHW051508070426
835507LV00022B/2995